LANGUAGE!®

The Comprehensive Literacy Curriculum

Assessment: Content Mastery

Book C

Jane Fell Greene, Ed.D.

SOPRIS WEST EDUCATIONAL SERVICES
A CAMBIUM LEARNING COMPANY

BOSTON, MA • NEW YORK, NY • LONGMONT, CO

13 14 15   HPS   13 12 11

Editorial Director: Nancy Chapel Eberhardt
Word and Phrase Selection: Judy Fell Woods
English Learners: Jennifer Wells Greene
Lesson Development: Sheryl Ferlito, Donna Lutz, Isabel Wesley
Morphology: John Alexander, Mike Minsky, Bruce Rosow
Text Selection: Sara Buckerfield, Jim Cloonan
Decodable and Independent Text: Jenny Hamilton, Steve Harmon

ISBN 10 Digit: 1-59318-296-1
ISBN 13 Digit: 978-1-59318-296-0

Printed in the United States of America

Published and distributed by

Cambium
L E A R N I N G®
Sopris West®

4093 Specialty Place • Longmont, CO 80504 • (303) 651-2829
www.sopriswest.com

70906/6-11

Table of Contents

Name _____

Syllable Awareness

Lesson 5 • Step 1

Listen to each word your teacher says. Repeat the word. Write the number of syllables in the first column. Write the number of vowel sounds in the second column.

	How many syllables are in the word?	How many vowel sounds are in the word?
1.		
2.		
3.		
4.		
5.		
6.		
7.		
8.		
9.		
10.		

Name _____

Spelling Posttest 1

Total Number
Correct _____ /15

Lesson 5 • Step 2

Write the words your teacher says.

1. _____   9. _____

2. _____   10. _____

3. _____   11. _____

4. _____   12. _____

5. _____   13. _____

6. _____   14. _____

7. _____   15. _____

8. _____

Word Relationships

Lesson 8 • Step 3

Listen to your teacher read the directions. Listen to the **bold** word pairs. Listen to your choices. Select the correct answer and fill in the bubble for that answer. Look at the example.

Example: Listen: **infant: blanket**
Are these words synonyms (same), antonyms (opposites), or attributes?

infant: blanket

○ A. same

○ B. opposites

○ C. attributes

Continue with the remaining items.

1. Listen: **second: minute**
Are these words synonyms (same), antonyms (opposites), or attributes?

second: minute

○ A. same

○ B. opposites

○ C. attributes

2. Listen: **bottom: base**
Are these words synonyms (same), antonyms (opposites), or attributes?

bottom: base

○ A. same

○ B. opposites

○ C. attributes

3. Listen: **solid: water**
Are these words antonyms (opposites), attributes, or neither?

solid: water

○ A. opposites

○ B. attributes

○ C. neither

4. Listen: **common: uncommon**
Are these words synonyms (same), antonyms (opposites), or attributes?

common: uncommon

○ A. same

○ B. opposites

○ C. attributes

5. Listen: **over: above**
Are these words synonyms (same), antonyms (opposites), or neither?

over: above

○ A. same

○ B. opposites

○ C. neither

Name _____

Prefixes

Lesson 8 • Step 3

Listen to your teacher read the sentences. Use the **Word Bank** to fill in the blanks.

Word Bank		
apart	into	opposite
prefix	not	away

1. A _____ is a syllable or word part added to the beginning of words.

2. The prefix **in-** can mean ___ or _____.

3. The prefixes **non-** and **un-** mean _____ .

4. The prefixes **dis-**, **non-**, and **un-** can change a word into its _____.

5. The prefix **dis-** can also mean _____ or _____.

Name _____

Spelling Posttest 2

Total Number
Correct _____ /15

Lesson 10 • Step 2

Write the words your teacher says.

1. _____

2. _____

3. _____

4. _____

5. _____

Helping Verbs

Lesson 10 • Step 4

Underline the verb phrase in each sentence. Write the helping verb on the line.

1. We were clapping during the song. _____
2. They will be singing with us. _____
3. She is singing with the others. _____
4. I am clapping for her. _____
5. You are singing after them. _____

Nouns or Pronouns

Read each sentence. Identify the noun or pronoun that is the **subject** of the sentence. Write the word on the line.

6. The people elect the judges. _____
7. The water dripped onto the steps. _____
8. We will collect them. _____
9. They disrupted the students. _____
10. The principal presents the ribbons. _____

Nouns and Pronouns as Direct Objects

Identify and underline the direct object in each sentence.
Write the underlined word in the correct column.

	Noun	Pronoun
11. They elect the judges.	_____	_____
12. The water helped the plants.	_____	_____
13. We will collect them.	_____	_____
14. The noise disrupted her.	_____	_____
15. The principal presents the ribbons.	_____	_____

Syllable Awareness

Lesson 5 • Step 1

Listen to each word your teacher says. Repeat the word. Write the number of syllables in the first column. Write the number of vowel sounds in the second column.

	How many syllables are in the word?	How many vowel sounds are in the word?
1.		
2.		
3.		
4.		
5.		
6.		
7.		
8.		
9.		
10.		

Name _____

Spelling Posttest 1

Total Number
Correct _____ /15

Lesson 5 • Step 2

Write the words your teacher says.

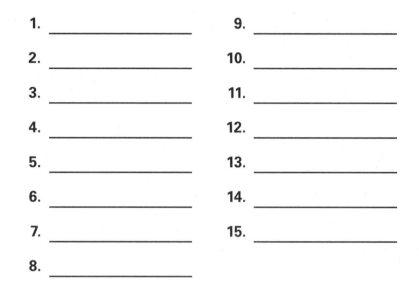

1. _____   9. _____

2. _____   10. _____

3. _____   11. _____

4. _____   12. _____

5. _____   13. _____

6. _____   14. _____

7. _____   15. _____

8. _____

Word Relationships

Lesson 8 • Step 3

Look at the **bold** word pairs. Listen to the choices. Select the correct answer and fill in the bubble for that answer. Look at the example.

> **Example:** Listen: **car: bumper**
> Are these words synonyms (same), antonyms (opposites), or attributes?
> **car: bumper**
> ○ A. same
> ○ B. opposites
> ○ C. attributes

Continue with the remaining items.

1. Listen: **day: morning**
Are these words synonyms (same), antonyms (opposites), or attributes?

day: morning

○ A. same

○ B. opposites

○ C. attributes

2. Listen: **twirl: spin**
Are these words synonyms (same), antonyms (opposites), or attributes?

twirl: spin

○ A. same

○ B. opposites

○ C. attributes

3. Listen: **river: current**
Are these words antonyms (opposites), attributes, or neither?

river: current

○ A. opposites

○ B. attributes

○ C. neither

4. Listen: **export: import**
Are these words synonyms (same), antonyms (opposites), or attributes?

export: import

○ A. same

○ B. opposites

○ C. attributes

5. Listen: **underpass: overpass**
Are these words synonyms (same), antonyms (opposites), or neither?

underpass: overpass

○ A. same

○ B. opposites

○ C. neither

Unit 14

Name _____

Morphology

Number Correct _____ /5

Lesson 8 • Step 3

Listen to your teacher read the sentences. Use the **Word Bank** to fill in the blanks.

Word Bank		
-er	suffixes	comparative
-est	superlative	adjective

1. The _____ -er and -est do a job when added to an _____.

2. The comparative suffix is _____ .

3. The superlative suffix is _____ .

4. The _____ suffix compares two things.

5. The _____ suffix compares more than two things or groups.

Total Number Correct _____ /10

Name _____

Spelling Posttest 2

Lesson 10 • Step 2

Write the words your teacher says.

1. _____

2. _____

3. _____

4. _____

5. _____

Name _____

Parts of Speech

Lesson 10 • Step 4

Read each sentence. Decide whether the underlined word is a noun, a verb, an adjective, or a preposition. Put an "X" in the correct column.

		Noun	Verb	Adjective	Preposition
1.	Cave artists made lots of sketches <u>inside</u> caves.				
2.	<u>Cave</u> artists made lots of sketches inside caves.				
3.	Cave artists made lots of sketches inside <u>caves</u>.				
4.	Artists sketched <u>crude</u> maps.				
5.	Artists <u>sketched</u> crude maps.				
6.	<u>Sketches</u> tell tales on cave walls.				
7.	Sketches tell tales <u>on</u> cave walls.				
8.	Artists in Mexico <u>painted</u> murals.				
9.	The <u>painted</u> murals had a purpose.				
10.	Walls are covered with beautiful <u>paintings</u>.				

Complete Subjects and Predicates

Read each sentence. Underline the complete subject once and the complete predicate twice.

11. Many cave artists made sketches on rock walls.

12. These sketches tell tales of long ago.

13. Cave dwellers left messages for others.

14. Mexican murals were painted in many colors.

15. Cave paintings served a useful purpose.

Name _____

Compound Subjects and Predicates

Lesson 10 • Step 4

Read each sentence. Decide which part of the sentence is compounded.
Put an "X" in the correct column. Circle the compounded sentence parts.

	Sentence	Compound Subject	Compound Predicate
16.	Yarn or twine can make fantastic art.		
17.	The cave dwellers hunted and fished.		
18.	Nutshells and caps became 3-D art.		
19.	People etched or drew marks on cave walls.		
20.	They sketched crude maps and made messages for each other.		

**Total Number
Correct _____ /20**

Name _____

Syllable Awareness

Total Number
Correct _____ /10

Lesson 5 • Step 1

Listen to your teacher say each word. Fill in the chart with the number of syllables and vowel sounds in each word.

	How many syllables are in the word?	How many vowel sounds are in the word?
1.		
2.		
3.		
4.		
5.		
6.		
7.		
8.		
9.		
10.		

Name _____

Spelling Posttest 1

Total Number
Correct _____/15

Lesson 5 • Step 2

Write the words your teacher says.

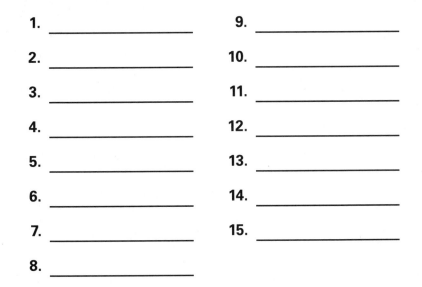

1. _____

2. _____

3. _____

4. _____

5. _____

6. _____

7. _____

8. _____

9. _____

10. _____

11. _____

12. _____

13. _____

14. _____

15. _____

Word Relationships

Lesson 8 • Step 3

Look at the **bold** word pairs. Listen to the choices. Select the correct answer and fill in the bubble for that answer. Look at the example.

> **Example:** Listen: **quiet: silent**
> Are these words synonyms (same), antonyms (opposites), or attributes?
> **quiet: silent**
>
> ○ A. synonyms
>
> ○ B. antonyms
>
> ○ C. attributes

Continue with the remaining items.

1. Listen: **defend: protect**
   Are these words synonyms (same), antonyms (opposites), or attributes?
   defend: protect

   ○ A. synonyms

   ○ B. antonyms

   ○ C. attributes

2. Listen: **hero: coward**
   Are these words synonyms (same), antonyms (opposites), or attributes?
   hero: coward

   ○ A. synonyms

   ○ B. antonyms

   ○ C. attributes

3. Listen: **unpack: repack**
   Are these words antonyms (opposites), attributes, or neither?
   unpack: repack

   ○ A. antonyms

   ○ B. attributes

   ○ C. neither

4. Listen: **supermarket: cart**
   Are these words synonyms (same), antonyms (opposites), or attributes?
   supermarket: cart

   ○ A. synonyms

   ○ B. antonyms

   ○ C. attributes

5. Listen: **tiger: lion**
   Are these words synonyms (same), antonyms (opposites), or neither?
   tiger: lion

   ○ A. synonyms

   ○ B. antonyms

   ○ C. neither

Name _____

Morphology

Lesson 8 • Step 3

Listen to your teacher read the sentences. Use the **Word Bank** to fill in the blanks.

Word Bank		
adjective	participle	suffix
noun	prefix	verb

1. **-ing** is a _____.

2. We can add the suffix **-ing** to a _____.

3. We call a verb with the suffix **-ing** added to it a present _____.

4. We can use the present participle to describe a _____.

5. A word that can describe or give more information about a noun

   is an _____.

Name _____

Spelling Posttest 2

Total Number
Correct _____ /15

Lesson 10 • Step 2

Write the words your teacher says.

1. _____

2. _____

3. _____

4. _____

5. _____

Name _____

Have—Main Verb or Helping Verb

| Number Correct | /5 |

Lesson 10 • Step 4

Read each sentence. Underline the form of the verb **have**. Decide if the form of **have** is used as a main verb or a helping verb. Fill in the correct bubble.

		Main Verb	Helping Verb
1.	The girls had success.	○	○
2.	The class has written a myth.	○	○
3.	Juan will have a big surprise.	○	○
4.	You have taken the first step.	○	○
5.	I have been here before.	○	○

Prepositions

| Number Correct | /10 |

Read each sentence. Read the underlined prepositional phrase. Circle the preposition. Decide if the preposition is indicating time or space. Put an "X" in the correct column.

Two points per item.

		Time	Space
6.	In the forest, fires burned many trees and homes.		
7.	Firefighters fought scorching heat and strong winds for hours.		
8.	During storms, lightning strikes trees and buildings.		
9.	The military trains soldiers and pilots in academies.		
10.	Fires inside the forest killed native birds and plants.		

Compound Direct Objects

Lesson 10 • Step 4

Read each sentence. Decide which part of the sentence is the compound direct object. Circle the compound direct object.

11. Jupiter and Neptune ruled the air and seas.

12. Today, people do not believe the myths and tales.

13. Only Neptune could calm the stormy seas and waves.

14. Police and firefighters protect our lands and property.

15. Men and women in the military preserve our peace and security.

Total Number
Correct _____ /20

Answering Questions

Lesson 10 • Step 5

Eskimos: Land and People

What do you know of the Eskimos' land? It is vast. It crosses Asia and North America. Much of the land is permanently frozen. It is often windy. Most of it is treeless. Yet the Eskimos call it the "Beautiful Land." This land has been their home for thousands of years.

The seasons bring different challenges to the Eskimo people. In winter, temperatures fall below 0°F. Sometimes, they dip below -50°F. For months, the sun never rises above the horizon. There are just a few hours of light each day. In contrast, summers are short. Daylight lasts 24 hours. Summer temperatures rise to around 40°F. Bogs and swamps dot the land. Many Eskimos use the summer months to hunt and gather food for the winter.

Modern inventions have brought changes to the old way of life. Snowmobiles have replaced dog sleds. Metal has replaced bone and stone tools. Television has replaced storytelling. Some Eskimos worry these changes will erase the Eskimo culture. Grandparents teach the children. They teach the stories and traditions of their ancestors. They teach the Eskimo languages. They practice the old arts and crafts. They encourage the children to respect the ways of the past.

---

1. What can you conclude about how the Eskimo people feel about their land?

_____

2. What can you generalize about life as an Eskimo during the winter?

_____

3. Identify one of the inventions that has brought change to Eskimo life.

_____

_____

_____

Answering Questions

Lesson 10 • Step 5

Four-Footed Hero

Date and time: New York City, September 11, 2001. Terrorists crashed two planes into the World Trade Center. Hundreds of heroes rushed into blazing buildings.

One hero was twelve years old. His name was Bear. He was a golden retriever. Bear and his owner, Captain Scott Shields, were on the scene 38 minutes after the first plane struck.

The first dog on site, Bear went straight to work. He used his powerful sense of smell. He found victims. He worked 22 hours a day for three straight days. Bear never gave up. He located three of the only five survivors in the debris.

In 2002, Bear died. In New York Harbor, a memorial service on the aircraft carrier *U.S.S. Intrepid* honored him.

---

4. Explain how Bear found the victims in the debris.

_____

5. What can you infer about why Bear was honored with a memorial service?

_____

_____

_____

_____

Name _____

Syllable Awareness

Lesson 5 • Step 1

Read each word. Fill in the chart with the number of syllables and vowel sounds in each word.

		How many syllables are in the word?	How many vowel sounds are in the word?
1.	excluded		
2.	suppose		
3.	creating		
4.	beside		
5.	presume		
6.	repetitive		
7.	homecoming		
8.	eradicate		
9.	revise		
10.	riverside		

Name _____

Spelling Posttest 1

Total Number
Correct _____ /15

Lesson 5 • Step 2

Write the words your teacher says.

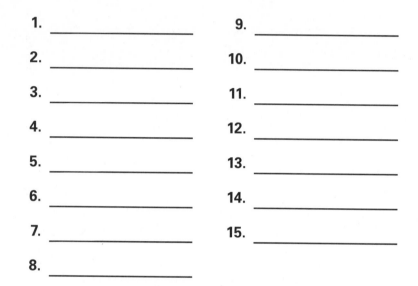

1. _____

2. _____

3. _____

4. _____

5. _____

6. _____

7. _____

8. _____

9. _____

10. _____

11. _____

12. _____

13. _____

14. _____

15. _____

Name _____

Word Relationships

Lesson 8 • Step 3

Read the analogy. Think about the relationship of word pairs. Choose a word pair that is the same relationship. Look at the example.

> **Example:** Listen: **arrive: depart** :: _____
> Finish the analogy.
>
>   ○ A. band: trombone
>   ○ B. include: exclude
>   ○ C. safe: secure

1. Listen: **parade: drum** :: _____
   Finish the analogy.
   ○ A. provide: give
   ○ B. polite: rude
   ○ C. band: trombone

2. Listen: **admire: respect** :: _____
   Finish the analogy.
   ○ A. safe: secure
   ○ B. complete: begin
   ○ C. band: trombone

3. Listen: **math: divide** :: _____
   Finish the analogy.
   ○ A. safe: secure
   ○ B. polite: rude
   ○ C. music: sing

4. Listen: **complete: begin** :: _____
   Finish the analogy.
   ○ A. create: make
   ○ B. polite: rude
   ○ C. storm: thunder

5. Listen: **athletes: compete** :: _____
   Finish the analogy.
   ○ A. safe: secure
   ○ B. arrive: depart
   ○ C. candidates: debate

Name _____

Morphology

Number
Correct _____ /5

Lesson 8 • Step 3

Listen to your teacher read the sentences. Use the **Word Bank** to fill in the blanks.

Word Bank			
adjective	participle	suffix	tense
-en	past	-ed	nouns

1. When **-ing** is added to a verb, the verb can act as an _____.

2. The **-ing** form of a verb is called a present _____.

3. When we can add _____ or _____ to a verb, the verb can act as an adjective.

4. We call a verb with the suffixes **-ed** or **-en** added to it a _____ participle.

5. The present and past _____ participles can modify _____.

Total Number
Correct _____ /10

Name _____

Spelling Posttest 2

Lesson 10 • Step 2

Write the words your teacher says.

1. _____

2. _____

3. _____

4. _____

5. _____

6. _____

Name _____

Plural and Possessive Nouns

Number
Correct _____ /5

Lesson 10 • Step 4

Read each sentence. Decide if the underlined word is a plural noun, a singular possessive noun, or a plural possessive noun. Fill in the correct bubble.

		Plural Noun	Singular Possessive	Plural Possessive
1.	Jack's brown jacket was brand new.	○	○	○
2.	Different events test the athletes' skills.	○	○	○
3.	The skaters' helmets broke in the crash.	○	○	○
4.	His sneakers are red, white, and blue.	○	○	○
5.	The team's win was amazing.	○	○	○

Prepositional Phrases

Number
Correct _____ /10

Two points per item.

Read the paragraph. Underline the prepositional phrase and circle its preposition. Draw a square around the object of the preposition.

6. The Special Olympics Games began with great fanfare. 7. The athletes marched around the oval track. 8. Above the marchers' heads, flags were waving. 9. In the hushed arena, all the athletes waited. 10. At the signal, the flame was lit and the first event started.

Compound Adjectives

Lesson 10 • Step 4

Read each sentence. Underline the compound adjective. Draw an arrow to the noun that the adjectives describe.

11. The male and female athletes took their places at the starting line.

12. The girl lost her silver and gold medals after the race.

13. Willing and devoted volunteers organize Special Olympics.

14. Sudden or unexpected stops injure extreme skaters.

15. Extreme athletes live risky but exciting lives.

Name _____

Syllable Awareness

Total Number
Correct _____ /10

Lesson 5 • Step 1

Read each word. Fill in the chart with the number of syllables and vowel sounds in each word.

		How many syllables are in the word?	How many vowel sounds are in the word?
1.	enzyme		
2.	synthetic		
3.	stormy		
4.	understandingly		
5.	myth		
6.	hybrid		
7.	priority		
8.	storytellers		
9.	army		
10.	typecasting		

Name _____

Spelling Posttest 1

Total Number
Correct _____ /15

Lesson 5 • Step 2

Write the words your teacher says.

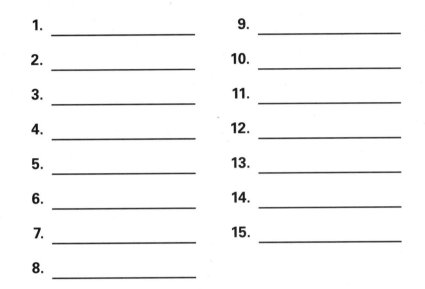

1. _____   9. _____

2. _____   10. _____

3. _____   11. _____

4. _____   12. _____

5. _____   13. _____

6. _____   14. _____

7. _____   15. _____

8. _____

Word Relationships

Lesson 8 • Step 3

Read the first analogy. Think about the relationship of word pairs. Choose a word that finishes the second analogy. Look at the example.

> **Example:**   Listen: **poor: broke ::**
> **silly:** _____
> Finish the analogy.
>
>   ○ A. sad
>   ○ B. funny
>   ○ C. shy

1. Listen: **ugly: pretty ::**
   compare: _____
   Finish the analogy.
     ○ A. conflict
     ○ B. contract
     ○ C. contrast

2. Listen: **North America: United States ::**
   Africa: _____
   Finish the analogy.
     ○ A. Nile River
     ○ B. Egypt
     ○ C. pyramid

3. Listen: **quickly: rapidly ::**
   timid: _____
   Finish the analogy.
     ○ A. shy
     ○ B. fast
     ○ C. ugly

4. Listen: **penny: money ::**
   byte: _____
   Finish the analogy.
     ○ A. dime
     ○ B. memory
     ○ C. twenty

5. Listen: **conflict: harmony ::**
   ruin: _____
   Finish the analogy.
     ○ A. sad
     ○ B. contrast
     ○ C. construct

Suffixes

Lesson 8 • Step 3

Listen to your teacher read the sentences. Use the **Word Bank** to fill in the blanks.

Word Bank				
-ly	adverbs	**-est**	adjective	**-er**
how	three	when	adverb	nouns

1. Adding _____ to an adjective changes the word to an _____.

2. _____ that end in **-ly** answer the questions _____.

3. Adding _____ signals comparison between two _____ or pronouns.

4. Adding _____ signals comparison among _____ nouns or pronouns.

5. We usually use the words **more** and **most** before a multisyllable _____.

Name _____

Spelling Posttest 2

Total Number
Correct _____ /15

Lesson 10 • Step 2

Write the words your teacher says.

1. _____

2. _____

3. _____

4. _____

5. _____

Name _____

Possessive Nouns

Lesson 10 • Step 4

Read each sentence. Change the underlined words into the possessive form. Write the possessive form on the line provided.

1. The riches of King Tut were buried in his tomb. _____

2. Some of the life of King Tut is still a mystery. _____

3. Today the rulers of Egypt are elected. _____

4. Scientists can reconstruct details of the lives of people. _____

5. The teeth of an older person are often ground down. _____

Adverbs

Read each sentence. Find and underline the adverb or adverbial phrase in each sentence. Decide if the underlined part tells *how*, *when*, or *where*. Put an "X" in the correct column.

		how	when	where
6.	In ancient Egypt, not many children were educated.			
7.	After death, bodies were mummified.			
8.	Dead bodies were treated respectfully and carefully.			
9.	Many treasures were found in King Tut's grave.			
10.	Scientists study a tomb's contents in great detail.			

Do—Main Verb or Helping Verb

Lesson 10 • Step 4

Read each sentence. Underline the verb or verb phrase in each sentence. Decide if the word **do** is used as a main verb or a helping verb. Fill in the correct bubble.

		Main Verb	Helping Verb
11.	Builders of the pyramids did follow a precise plan.	◯	◯
12.	Scientists will be doing more research on the pyramids.	◯	◯
13.	Young boys in ancient Egypt did many jobs.	◯	◯
14.	They were doing their tasks really well.	◯	◯
15.	A stonecutter does carve quickly.	◯	◯

Indirect Objects

Read each sentence. Find and underline the indirect object.

16. I will give you my notes for the pyramid test.

17. The teacher handed us the test in the morning.

18. She offered students a prize for the best results.

19. My mother lent me her favorite pen for the test.

20. The teacher gave the class its results.

Total Number Correct _____ /20

Name _____

Spelling Posttest 1

Lesson 5 • Step 2

Write the words your teacher says.

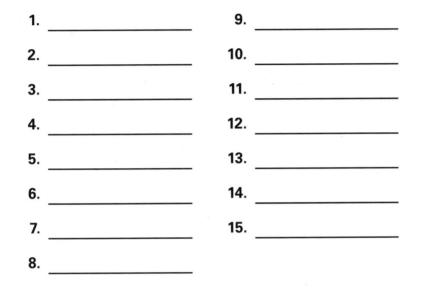

1. _____   9. _____

2. _____   10. _____

3. _____   11. _____

4. _____   12. _____

5. _____   13. _____

6. _____   14. _____

7. _____   15. _____

8. _____

Name _____

Spelling Posttest 2

Lesson 10 • Step 2

Write the words your teacher says.

1. _____

2. _____

3. _____

4. _____

   _____

5. _____